Sheffield At Play

Written and compiled by Andy Waple

First published in 2006 by:

At Heart Publications
32 Stamford Street,
Altrincham,
Cheshire, WA14 1EY

in conjunction with

The Star,
York Street,
Sheffield, S1 1PU

Images and text:
The Star (Sheffield) unless otherwise stated.

ISBN: 1-84547-108-3

Contents

Introduction

Sheffield has a long-held reputation of being a friendly city - a place where visitors are often surprised when they are spoken to by complete strangers.

One of the reasons for such relaxed openness may be that in a working class Northern city, Sheffielders have had to rely on each other for support during some tough times. Yet Sheffielders have always known how to enjoy themselves. And they haven't always required the hi-tech sophistication of the modern leisure industry to have fun.

Sheffield is full of folk who know how to smile without spending money. Of course, thousands of people from many generations have enjoyed visits to the pub, the cinema or simply to the shops. But there are many more who have derived great pleasure from trips to the local park to feed the ducks or simply by taking in the greenery for which Sheffield is so well known.

This book aims to show some of the many activities that Sheffield folk have enjoyed. Most of the pictures come from the three decades leading up to the turn of the century, and it is a far from exhaustive collection.

The heyday of the city's many parks are showcased to demonstrate that fun can be free. Sheffield's rolling hills and its river valleys are dotted with urban parks and woodland. Its borders contain more countryside and farmland than most comparable centres of population.

The pleasures of the popular Peace Gardens are an obvious inclusion. These are located on the original site of the churchyard of St Paul's, which was demolished to make way for a proposed extension to the Town Hall. The outbreak of the Second World War put an end to the project, so Sheffield Corporation laid out a "temporary" garden which was destined to become one of Sheffield's most enduring landmarks.

They were originally named St Paul's Gardens, but became known locally as The Peace Gardens, a name formally adopted in 1985 in the presence of a group of survivors of the Hiroshima Atom Bomb explosion. The Peace Gardens were completely rebuilt in 1998 as the first part of 'The Heart of the City' regeneration project.

Festivals and carnivals have long held a special place in Sheffielders' hearts, and for many years the Sheffield Show was a major event on many families' "must do" list. The Lord Mayor's Parade, with its floats passing through the city centre, has always attracted the crowds, and was boosted in the 1990s by the addition of the colourful and noisy Children's Festival.

Mention must be made of Sheffield Students' Rag Week. Twikker was Britain's groundbreaking "Rag Mag" when it was first produced in 1925 and it has

since been much copied up and down the country's campuses. Sheffield's first Rag is said to date back to the 1880s but the origin of the expression "rag" is clouded in disagreement.

Much of the students' fundraising is done behind the scenes, but various activities have found their way into Sheffield folklore. The most memorable events have been the Rag Day parade - led by the most hairy of fairies - and the raft races on the River Don. The notorious Pyjama Jump was all part of the fun until it was stopped for safety reasons.

People with more refined tastes when it comes to enjoying their leisure time have turned to the traditional venues of culture and the arts, from concert halls and theatres to galleries and museums.

Sheffield has a long history of theatre and by the turn of the 21st Century it had firmly cemented itself as a regional capital of culture. Many people have enjoyed an evening at the renowned Crucible and Lyceum Theatres that have both become landmarks in the city centre.

Dear to everybody's heart has always been the City Hall. Possibly Sheffield's best-loved building, it has been the memorable venue for a huge range of activities from orchestral music, pop, light entertainment, history and science lectures, to pantomime, dances and a whole host of other events.

Shopping turned from a necessity to recreation during the latter half of the last century. The likes of canned tongue and sterilised milk from the corner shop gave way to convenience food in the supermarkets and the range of consumer goods from clothing to electronics zoomed. No longer was shopping a grind - it was now a great day out for many in town or at Meadowhall.

One common factor of Sheffielders at play over the decades has been the pull of pubs and clubs as an aid to letting off steam or simply relaxing after a day at work or with the kids.

Pubs have remained as strong as ever and have witnessed the rise and fall of the Working Men's Club. Nightclubbing and dancing have survived the passing trends of changing generations and the city has held a long reputation as a great place for nightlife.

This is Sheffield at Play as seen from the archives of The Star's photographic treasure trove of a library - hardly a comprehensive view, but a snapshot of its citizens who have always known how to enjoy life to the full.

Andrew Wyple

Arts and Culture

The Crucible opened in
1971 as a replacement for
the Playhouse Theatre

Local boy Bobby Knutt became a household name in the 1980s with a series of sparkling panto performances. Here he is as Wishee Washee in Aladdin at the Crucible Theatre in 1980.

The Stirrings in Sheffield on a Saturday Night was a box office hit for the Crucible in 1982

Sally Ann Triplett in Cabaret, a Crucible success of the 1990s

"Knutty" again, this time with Sheffield star Marti Caine, in
Snow White and the Seven Dwarfs at the Lyceum Theatre

The cast of the
Wizard of Oz at the
Crucible

The Lyceum
Theatre
before
restoration

Atmospheric
shot of the
restoration of
the Lyceum
taken in 1989

The Lyceum Theatre restored to its former glory

Part of the Lyceum's magnificently restored interior

Sheffield theatreland at night

Sheffield's musical
tradition has a long
history. It's
demonstrated here by
1992 Young
Musicians of the Year,
Orhan Ahiskal and
Karen Slack.

These wrestlers at the City Museum scared generations of kids. The venue underwent a multi million pound refurbishment during 2005-06.

Everybody wanted to stroke Janie the Canadian Polar bear. Janie was renamed Snowy during the Museum's refit.

City Hall

Enter Hall by Door

City (Oval) Hall, Sheffield

C

THE WHO SHOW

Saturday, 28th October, 1967

FIRST HOUSE

at **6.20** p.m.

Doors open at 6.0 p.m.

BALCONY 6/6

(Side Entrance BALM GREEN)

SEAT **D**
Row

No. **30**

Booking Agents: Wilson Peck Ltd.

City (Oval) Hall Sheffield

Stringfellow Bros. present
in Concert II

FLEETWOOD MAC

MICK ABRAHAMS BLONDWIN PIG

Tuesday, 18th March, 1969

AT **8.00. P.M.**

Doors open at 7.30 p.m.

BALCONY 10/-

(SIDE ENTRANCE BALM GREEN)

SEAT **C 11**
Row

Booking Agents: Wilson Peck Ltd

CITY (OVAL) HALL - SHEFFIELD

BOOKING AGENT: WILSON PECK LTD.

CHRYSALIS PRESENTS

LED ZEPPELIN IN PERSON

FRIDAY, JANUARY 16th, 1970

at 8-0 p.m. Doors open 7-30 p.m.

BALCONY 10/6

SIDE ENTRANCE BALM GREEN

DOOR **C**

E 32

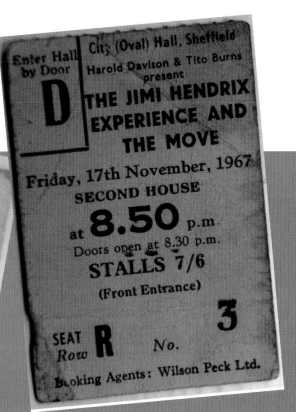

City (Oval) Hall, Sheffield

Enter Hall by Door

Harold Davison & Tito Burns present

D THE JIMI HENDRIX EXPERIENCE AND THE MOVE

Friday, 17th November, 1967

SECOND HOUSE

at **8.50** p.m.

Doors open at 8.30 p.m.

STALLS 7/6

(Front Entrance)

SEAT **R** No. **3**
Row

Booking Agents: Wilson Peck Ltd.

City (Oval) Hall, Sheffield

Bryan Morrison Agency presents

THE PINK FLOYD

(STEREO CONCERT)

Saturday, 24th May, 1969

AT **8.00**. P.M.

Doors open at 7.30 p.m.

STALLS 7/6

SEAT **G 16**
Row

ENTER HALL BY DOOR **K**

Booking Agents: Wilson Peck Ltd

Legendary acts rocked at the City Hall to full houses

CITY (OVAL) HALL - SHEFFIELD

BOOKING AGENT: WILSON PECK LTD.

JOHN and TONY SMITH present

Eric Clapton

Delany and Bonnie and Friends

Thursday, December 4th, 1969

at 8-50 p.m. Doors open 8-30

BALCONY 10/6

SIDE ENTRANCE BALM GREEN

DOOR **C** **C47**

A 1952 brochure painted a picture of gentile elegance in the foyer

A young City
Hall shown from
Cambridge
Street in 1932

The building before
pedestrianisation of
Barker's Pool, 1964

The interior of the Oval Hall with its two carved lions on stage. They were removed in 1968 after complaints from some performers that they put them off!

The City Hall's imposing size is evident in this picture from 1964

The City Hall from afar. The long-gone Grand Hotel, on Balm Green, and the former Cinema House on Barker's Pool are also visible.

Ballroom tea dances have long been a tradition and have remained popular over the years

A couple strut their stuff at one of the Hall's regular tea dances

More images of local folk enjoying a dance at the City Hall

Ballet star Rudolf Nureyev arrives at the City Hall in 1991 just two years before his death

A Night on the Town

Traditional pleasures: A fag and a pint down at the local

Irish night at Fagan's, Broad Lane

Thousands of publicans have served and entertained Sheffield's drinkers over the years. Among them were Michael and Kath Sullivan, who ran the Red House - known fondly as the "Irish Embassy" - on Solly Street.

Girls' night out at the pub

The Mojo Club, Pitsmoor, was the most popular nightspot for the flower-power generation of the 1960s

Clubbers from all over the city were attracted to The Mojo in Pitsmoor. It operated from 1964 until 1967 when it was boarded up prior to demolition.

The Fiesta was one of the
most successful nightclubs
of the 1970s

A night out at Romeo and Juliet's nightclub, 1983

Friday night out in 1994

Sheffield became a clubbing capital during the 1990s

Place your bets: a croupier sharpens her skills at Napoleon's Casino

Working Men's Clubs,
such as this one at
Woodseats, became
important meeting places
for local communities
across the city

Eyes down for bingo at the club

Crookes
Working Men's
Club, 1977

Card games and snooker - a typical night out for thousands in the 1970s

Called to the Bar
- Holbrook and
Halfway Working
Men's Club

Hackenthorpe Social Club

Some Working Men's Clubs turned to featuring female strippers in an attempt to halt flagging membership

Let's Dance

Ceroc dancing craze hits Orchard Square in 1993

Finalists limber up for a City Hall competition

Scratch Mix
breakdancer in
a spin

Street Crew breakdancers

Morris Men dancing in the street at
Grenoside 1984

Rock 'n' rollers at the hop

Dancers Lucy Melvin (left) and Katy Bush, aged seven...

...and still together in 1996

The Pagan tradition of maypole dancing played out at Bolsterstone Free School in 1986

Rachel Fisher jumps for joy

Strike a pose:
Charmaine Cross of
Parson Cross

David Kent and
Doreen Mullen
jiving at the Court
School of Dancing,
Abbeydale, 1976

Up the Blades! Grenoside Sword Dancers

Parklife

Rock Festival in Weston Park, 1979

Easy does it...
watching the
bowling in
Crookes Valley
Park, 1966

How many
children can
you get on a
roundabout?
Crookes Valley
Park, 1976

Locals make the most of the good weather in Weston Park

Sunbathing in the Peace Gardens before its remodelling

Feeding the pigeons in the Peace Gardens 1971

Three-year-old Jennie Dibb feeding the ducks, Endcliffe Park, 1974

The Peace Gardens have always been a popular spot for courting couples

If you can't beat 'em, join 'em! When the council stopped maintaining parks properly, local communities stepped in. Here are volunteers of the Friends of Porter Valley.

The National
Finals of the
Model Power Boat
Association,
Crookes Valley
Park, 1976

Messing about in boats, High Hazels Park, Darnall, 1971

Phew! What a scorcher. Cooling down on a hot summer's day, courtesy of the parky. Parson Cross Park, 1975.

Hillsborough Park, 1910

Feeding frenzy, Bingham Park 1984

Girls take to the ice at
Wiremill Dam, 1961

The ice is back and
this time Martin Glew
is shown the ropes by
sister Susan and her
friend Angela Nunn

The Star's "Auntie Janet" releases a duckling in Endcliffe Park, 1980, after a spate of vandalism reduced their numbers

Little swingers, Chelsea Park, 1990

The famous stepping stones over the River Porter, Endcliffe Park

Tall boys and a girl rise to the occasion in Stannington Park, 1975

Monty the Clown from the BBC's Multi-Coloured Swap Shop entertains kids in Norfolk Park, 1981

The Bandstand at Firth Park, about 1910

We are sailing: a beautiful model yacht glides across Wire Mill Dam

Boys inspect the
army's firepower on
display at the Sheffield
Show in Hillsborough
Park, 1974

Pond Dipping at Wire Mill Dam

This Sporting Life

Step aerobics, here at
Ponds Forge, became
a fitness craze of the
1990s

It was hardly the Mediterranean, but Crookesmoor Park was good enough for these imaginative windsurfers in 1989

Did you think the Sheffield Marathon was a recent introduction? Here it is in 1946

A gentle game of bowls in the park

One-ers at the ready! The boys of Birkdale School get down to the annual conker fight

Preparing for battle - Kevin Hutchinson and Mark Dawes

Public swimming was provided by the Victorians who built Glossop Road Baths and others. Pictured is a swimming lesson at Glossop Road in 1956.

The Sheaf Valley Baths were infamous for being a few hairs' breadth short of Olympic standards

But it had what others lacked - a mural painted by Rolf Harris!

Ponds Forge brought a day out at the baths up to a new level of luxury

The swimming pool became the finest in Britain
when it opened with a fanfare in 1991

The 147 Club at Ecclesfield in 1986. The snooker craze in Sheffield was fuelled by the interest in The Embassy World Championships, held annually at the Crucible since 1976.

And the craze didn't confine itself to the men

Broomgrove club team won the Sheffield Amateur Snooker Club B teams section in 1984

Local challenger Shaun Farrell pitted his cue against the might of professional Rex Williams at the Springwood Hotel, Hastilar Road South, in 1986

Langton's team made The Star Cup
Final at Darnall Liberal Club in 1992

Brian Abdul
found a way of
joining the
snooker craze
despite having
lost his left arm

David Martin and
Eugene Hughes
dressed smartly for
a gentlemanly game
of snooker in 1980

Sue Ward was the first
woman to play in the
Sheffield Works Snooker
League in 1979

You're never too old
to learn how to swim
- a pensioners'
swimming lesson led
by Rose Gore in 1976

Sheffield's
Peak District -
here at
Burbage Edge
- is a rock
climber's
paradise

BMX biker shows a clean pair of wheels

Real snow at Sheffield Ski Village, 1996

Mogul jumping
at the Sheffield
Ski Village

Snowboarding
on the piste

Leisure pursuits old and
new - anglers on the banks
of Sheffield Canal with the
Arena emerging in the
background

Fore! The Sheffield
Veterans Golf Society
tee off at Wortley
Golf Club

Shopping

Shopping has always been a popular leisure activity. This is the logo for the pre-Christmas Shopping Festival in 1961.

Max Factor
girl in action,
1961

Christmas shopping in Fargate

Service with a smile....

Castle Market used to attract crowds of bargain hunters. After years of decline it was due to relocate to a new market hall off The Moor.

Ghettoblaster from the past being demonstrated at Wilson Peck in 1961

Lipton's self service came to Haymarket in 1957, bringing shopping trolleys and revolutionising shopping

What is it about women and shoes? Here they are checking the latest stilettos in 1963…

…and the jewellery in 1969

Getting stocked up for Christmas with canned meat and fruits was essential for many people

Sale fever and a rush to get Dr Scholl exercise sandals, which were all the rage in 1976

Meadowhall with its free car parking and indoor malls brought renewed pleasure to shopping

The giant Meadowhall centre under construction

A helicopter lowers the cupola onto the main dome at Meadowhall

Meadowhall shopping mecca

Sheila Gray opens
Meadowhall on
4 September 1990

Shoppers pour into the
newly opened malls

Shopping frenzy at Meadowhall

Out and About

Mucking about on the water
became a popular pastime with the
restoration of the Sheffield and
South Yorkshire Navigation Canal.
Victoria Quays became a location
for people with waterborne homes.

Black lambs,
Nelson and
Mandela, were
born at Whirlow
Hall Farm Trust
- a wonderful
venue for
Sheffield's
children

The Friends of Botanical
Gardens hard at work during
the early days of the
restoration of the
masterpiece

Tossing the pancake, at the same event

Pancake racing in hot
pants, Woodhouse,
Shrove Tuesday, 1975

Hold on tight! Sheffield's famous hills are fantastic for winter sledging

Old Sheffield Heritage: folk watch grinding at Shepherd Wheel in Bingham Park

Oh for the quiet life...spinners at the wheel, Sheffield Show, 1989

All the fun of the fair...Oakes Park Fun Fair mud bath

Snakes alive! Who would wear this as a feather boa? Diane Griffin of Claywood Drive went for the real thing.

Heeley City Farm is a great draw for children and adults across the city. Here, Sarah Omelia, aged 7, prepares for a ride on the donkey.

Hats off to
Sheffield
Barbershop
Harmony
Group…

... and the girls
gave voice too -
Sheffield Ladies'
Barbershop
Harmony Group

"Long Live the Queen": a street party in Ferrars Close, Tinsley, celebrates the Queen's Silver Jubilee in 1977

Inspecting the wine cellar stock. For many years, The Sheffield Club was the watering hole of the city's gentry.

Festivals

A street party
on the Wicker,
1977, to
celebrate the
Queen's Silver
Jubilee

Mother Earth and other
creatures emerge from Sir
Harold Jackson School as
children prepare for the 1992
Sheffield Festival

Chess game in the Upper Sanctuary Gardens, Norfolk Street during the same event

Give us a twirl - Ukraine Cossack dancers and musicians in Tudor Square performing for the 1992 Sheffield Festival

Lord Mayor's Parade floats travel up High Street in 1968

Lady Komedie entertaining
by-passers in Tudor Square

Catalan Giants
dwarf all before
them in Fargate

Festival Parade preview, Silverdale School, 1992

Glamour among the
flower beds: Lord
Mayor's Parade, 1973

Lord Mayor's Parade passes
seated dignitaries in 1974.
The old Wilson Peck Music
Shop is on the corner.

The rare sight of a Lancaster bomber, Hurricane and Spitfire fighters over the Town Hall in 1983 for the Lord Mayor's Parade

"On yer bike" - 33 girls from Tommy Ward's get ready to pedal to the Lord Mayor's Parade in 1975

Pole dancing, 1975 style, at the Sheffield Spectacular

Salesgirl of the Year,
Kathleen Umlouf, with Lady
Sales Assistant of the Year,
Judith McCabe, at the 1975
Lord Mayor's Parade

Whoa! Annie Oakleys and a cowboy holding on tight at Sheffield Show, 1974

Doreen May with her dolls at Sheffield Show 1986. Sales proceeds went to Weston Park Hospital.

Ouch! A prickly customer keeps Paul Collinson at bay at the 1983 Sheffield Show

Sheffield students' traditional Rag
Week is a highly successful
charity fundraising jamboree led
by hundreds of students with their
collecting tins, and supported by
thousands from a highly amused
public. These "nurses" were
preparing for their parade in 1973.

The Rag Day procession - the highlight of the week - on High Street in 1973, watched by hundreds of onlookers

Acting crazy was all part of the fun on this float in 1976

Traditionally, the rag procession has been led by a male "fairy". Here's social science undergraduate Chris Pockert ready for action in 1970.

Fairy Andrew Hind on Church Street in 1974

The fairy was accompanied by "Mrs Mop" the following year

It is a tradition for the Lord Mayor to buy the first copy of the rag magazine, Twikker, from the fairy on the Town Hall steps

On with the Show!

Billy Smart's "Jungalero Spectacular" thrilled audiences in Hillsborough Park when the circus came to town in 1970

Billy Smart's superman, Markus, juggles artillery shell cases during the show

The ABC cinema, Snig Hill, in 1965. It was showing 'The Hill', starring Sean Connery, Harry Andrews and Michael Redgrave. Next door is the famous Cockaynes department store.

The Old Gaumont cinema in Barker's Pool, 1953, showing 'What Price Glory'

Darnall Grenadiers Band before the march

Torvill and Dean cutting the ice at Sheffield Arena

Sheffield Arena, later known as the
Hallam FM Arena, brought a new era
of leisure-time enjoyment to Sheffield

"The Full Monty" film made
Sheffield famous years after this
hunk entertained the girls on West
Street at the Limit Club in 1984